Earth Scientists:

From Mercator to Evans

by Lynn Van Gorp

Science Contributor
Sally Ride Science
Science Consultants
Nancy McKeown, Planetary Geologist
William B. Rice, Engineering Geologist

First hardcover edition published in 2009 by
Compass Point Books
151 Good Counsel Drive
P.O. Box 669
Mankato, MN 56002-0669

Editor: Mari Bolte
Designer: Heidi Thompson
Editorial Contributor: Sue Vander Hook

Art Director: LuAnn Ascheman-Adams
Creative Director: Joe Ewest
Editorial Director: Nick Healy
Managing Editor: Catherine Neitge

 This book was manufactured with paper containing at least 10 percent post-consumer waste.

Van Gorp, Lynn.
  Earth scientists : from Mercator to Evans / by Lynn Van Gorp. —1st hardcover ed.
    p. cm — (Mission. Science)
  Includes index.
  ISBN 978-0-7565-4235-1 (library binding)
  1. Geologists—Biography—Juvenile literature.
  2. Geographers—Biography—Juvenile literature. I. Title. II. Series.
  QE21.V36 2009
  550.92'2—dc22   2009002820

Visit Compass Point Books on the Internet at *www.compasspointbooks.com*
or e-mail your request to *custserv@compasspointbooks.com*

Table of Contents

Extraordinary Earth

Earth is an extraordinary place. If you explored the planet, you would see spreading plains, snow capped mountains, and deep gorges with swiftly flowing rivers. You might discover winding canyons, sandy beaches, icy glaciers, or rolling desert dunes.

People have explored landforms for thousands of years. They have wondered what Earth is made of and how it came to be. People who study the planet are called earth scientists. Most earth scientists specialize in one aspect of our world, such as rocks, soil, oceans, or glaciers. Others study how gravity and magnetism affect the planet. Still others investigate the climate or life-forms that live on Earth.

Ancient Landforms

The ancient Greeks and Romans studied landforms and recorded the changes that took place in the land around them. Their writings included details about erosion and earthquakes. In 550 B.C. the Greek philosopher Anaximander, known as the founder of scientific geography, drew the first map of the entire known world.

Although Anaximander's original map was lost, ancient writers ▶ who saw the map have described it in their works.

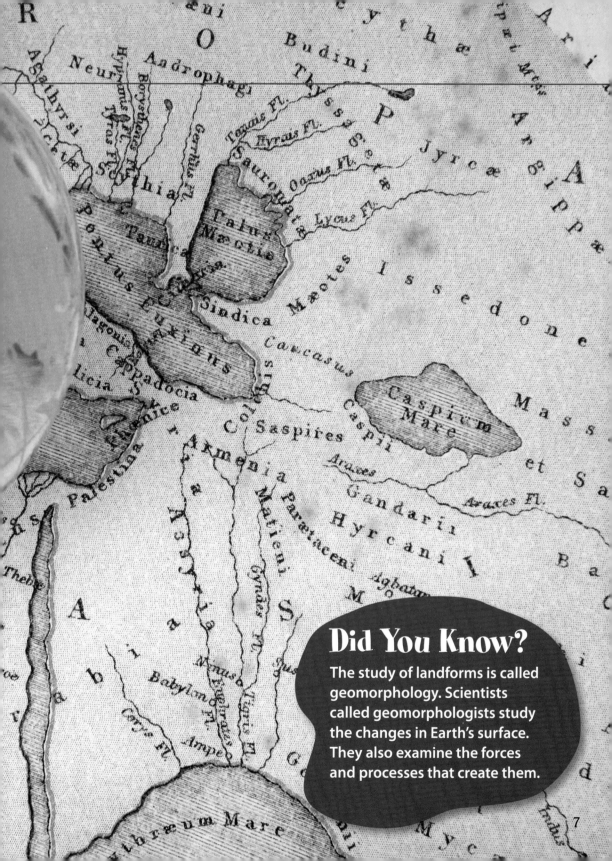

Did You Know?

The study of landforms is called geomorphology. Scientists called geomorphologists study the changes in Earth's surface. They also examine the forces and processes that create them.

Throughout history, earth scientists have charted their findings on maps. Maps were one of the best ways that people could record what the land was like. Maps are still important when studying Earth.

Gerardus Mercator was one of the most well known mapmakers of all time. His skill as an engraver of brass plates got him involved in mapmaking. When he was 23 years old, two cartographers—mapmakers—asked him to construct a brass globe.

Within two years, Mercator was making his own maps: one of Palestine, one of Flanders, where he was born, and another of the world. His world map was a projection, with the globe spread out on a flat surface. Projection maps have problems, though. The size and shape of the land near the poles are not correct, and Europe and North America look much bigger than Africa. In fact Africa is much bigger than both of them combined.

When Mercator was 40, he opened his own cartography workshop. At first he made his world globes by carving a sphere out of wood or brass. It was a time-consuming task, and he could only make one globe at a time. He came up with a new process so many globes could be made at once.

Mercator started with a wooden model that he covered with papier mâché. Next he glued a printed world map onto the mold. He inserted caps where the map came together at the poles. Finally he hand-painted the globe with watercolors and set it in a wooden stand. Today most globes are made by machines, but they still use Mercator's basic idea.

Maps and globes are very important to earth scientists. They can depict the lay of the land and guide people to where they want to go.

Did You Know?

Globes that depict Earth are called terrestrial globes. Globes that depict the sky are called celestial globes.

Maps vs. Globes

A map is a two-dimensional view of Earth, while a globe is a three-dimensional model. Globes are the only way Earth can be shown as it really is. Flat maps are useful, but they are not completely accurate.

John Wesley Powell (1834–1902)

John Wesley Powell is best known for his exploration of the Grand Canyon. Powell was born in Mount Morris, New York, in 1834. From an early age, he had an adventuresome nature. He liked to explore and collect things. His family moved several times, so he was able to experience the United States, including Ohio, Wisconsin, and Illinois, where he attended college.

In his early 20s, Powell went on several adventure trips. The first was a four-month walk across the state of Wisconsin to study wildlife and landforms. The following year, he rowed a boat down the Mississippi River from Minnesota to the Gulf of Mexico. He made similar expeditions on the Ohio and Illinois rivers.

During the Civil War (1861–1865), Powell served in the Union Army. He lost an arm during one battle, but that didn't stop him. When the war ended, he began teaching geology at Illinois Wesleyan University. Then his curious nature took him back to exploring.

In 1869, with nine other men, four boats, and a 10-month supply of food, he set out to explore the Grand Canyon. The swift waters of the Colorado River were more than he bargained for, however, and not all the boats and food made it through. Four men left the expedition. But Powell believed he could make it through the Grand Canyon, and at the end of three

months, the remaining six men emerged at the mouth of the Virgin River.

Powell took note of what he saw along the way. He believed erosion caused by the Colorado River had formed the canyon. Two years later he made the trip again. This time he made a map of the area.

When Powell was 49, he helped establish the United States Geological Survey. The USGS, which still exists today, focuses on earth science, including changes in landforms, natural resources, and natural hazards.

Powell worked with the Paiute tribe on his second expedition.

The Grand Canyon is 277 miles (446 kilometers) long.

to Florida. Then, on a trip to California, he visited Yosemite Valley in the Sierra Nevada mountains. He was inspired by its towering granite mountains, giant sequoia trees, and the overall beauty of the landforms. Today Yosemite is a national park, recognized as a special landform and protected by the United States.

Muir spent the rest of his life working outdoors, exploring and trying to preserve the beauty of nature. He also came up with ideas about how landforms developed, suggesting that glaciers had shaped many valleys. It was a new idea for his time and one that was not accepted by many. Muir died December 24, 1914, at the age of 76.

Like John Wesley Powell, John Muir was an avid adventurer. He was born in Scotland, but his family immigrated to the United States in 1849. While taking a botany course at the University of Wisconsin in Madison, Muir became interested in nature. He didn't graduate from the university, but rather set out on grand expeditions to study the country's landscape and plant life.

On his first trip, Muir walked the 1,000 miles (1,610 km) from Indiana

Sierra Club

The Sierra Club, founded in 1892 by John Muir, is dedicated to exploring and preserving nature. It encourages people to protect and restore the natural environment.

Yosemite National Park was one of the first wilderness parks in the United States. Between 1850 and 1860, fewer than 650 people traveled to Yosemite. Today more than 3.5 million people visit the park each year.

Other Protected Landforms

- Ayers Rock in Australia, the world's largest monolith, a tall block of stone that stands by itself
- Mount Fuji in Japan, an active volcano and Japan's highest mountain
- The Galapagos Islands off the coast of Ecuador, made of six large islands and several smaller islands; some of the volcanoes that formed these islands are still active
- Machu Picchu in Peru, an ancient city high in the Andes mountains and one of the world's most amazing ruins; it has been called the Lost City of the Incas.
- The Great Barrier Reef in Australia, with more than 2,800 coral reefs; the reefs are being damaged by the effects of human activities, but scientists are working hard to protect them
- Carlsbad Caverns in New Mexico, with more than 80 remarkable caves that feature spectacular mineral formations

New York native Grove Karl Gilbert studied Greek and math in the hopes of becoming a teacher. But he soon discovered a new line of work. After working at a science center studying fossils, rocks, minerals, and other aspects of Earth's surface, he knew that geology was what he wanted to study. He dedicated the rest of his life to studying the land—how it was formed and how it was changing.

In 1874, at the age of 31, Gilbert joined one of John Wesley Powell's expeditions to the Rocky Mountains. When the USGS was created in 1879, Gilbert was appointed senior geologist.

Twenty years later, a wealthy railroad owner named E.H. Harriman took 126 scientists and artists aboard an ocean liner to explore the coast of Alaska. Gilbert was one of the scientists chosen for the trip, which was the largest scientific expedition up to that time.

Many of the scientists studied the plants and animals of the region. Gilbert studied the glaciers and landforms. More than 5,000 photographs were taken to record their findings. On his return, Gilbert wrote a book about his explorations. Many people thought it was the best account of the trip.

In 1905 Gilbert went to California to study gold mining. He had always wanted to feel an earthquake, and in 1906 he got his wish. That year the great San Francisco earthquake hit. Gilbert felt its power, and he saw its destruction. For months he studied the damages and causes of the disaster. Gilbert continued to work for the USGS until his death in 1918 at the age of 75.

Deadly Earthquakes

The San Francisco earthquake of 1906 is considered one of the United States' worst natural disasters. Around 3,000 people died in the quake and fire that followed. More than 28,000 buildings were lost, leaving 225,000 people homeless. The earth shook from Los Angeles to Oregon and east to central Nevada.

In 2004 an undersea earthquake hit the Indian Ocean, triggering gigantic tsunamis. The waves killed more than 225,000 people in 11 countries. The hardest hit were Indonesia, Sri Lanka, India, and Thailand. The quake was the second largest earthquake ever recorded on a seismograph, with a magnitude between 9.1 and 9.3. The entire planet vibrated from its force, causing other earthquakes around the globe.

Did You Know?

The San Francisco earthquake lasted less than a minute. Some cracks left by the earthquake were 28 feet (8.5 meters) wide.

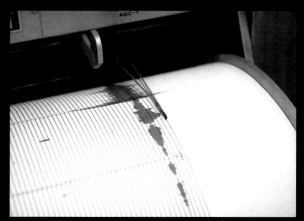

Seismographs show and record the power (magnitude) of earthquakes. Major earthquakes are rated at magnitudes of 7 or above.

William Morris Davis was interested in the world around him from a very young age. While his father was fighting in the Civil War, Davis was raised by his mother and grandmother in Philadelphia, Pennsylvania.

When he was 19, Davis received a master of engineering degree from Harvard University. Ten years later, he became a geology instructor there. Davis was also an explorer. For three years he worked at an observatory in South America, studying outer space. But his main interest was geology and geography, which had not been widely studied until that time. Davis wanted to change that. He thought everyone should know about our planet.

Modern technology in observatories allows us to see even farther and more clearly than ever before into the heavens.

owl nesting
in cactus

gila monster

kit fox
in burrow

ant

ant lion

A block diagram shows
the area beneath the
surface of the land.

Davis helped make geography a school subject. He thought students should know more than the names of places and where they are found. He wanted them to study landforms and how changes occur on Earth.

Davis also helped scientists learn a new way to observe and record their research by using maps and block diagrams. Block diagrams show a piece of something as though it had been cut like a slice of cake, showing what's inside. A block diagram of a hillside depicts the layers of soil and rock beneath the surface soil.

Davis studied a variety of landforms and described how he thought they had been created. He observed how rivers can change the landscape to make new landforms. He called this process the cycle of erosion. Geologists today know that the cycle of erosion has a lot to do with Earth's changing surface.

Davis' Cycle of Erosion

The cycle of erosion that Davis described has three time periods: youth, maturity, and old age. When mountains are first formed, they are considered to be young, with high, jagged surfaces. Then flowing water begins to create a V-shaped valley.

Over time the flowing water makes the valley wider and deeper. This stage is called maturity. In time mountains can become gently rolling hills, eroded by time, wear, wind, and water. This period is called old age.

Later two more processes were added to Davis' cycle: base level and rejuvenation. Some mountains wear down until all that is left is a flat, level plain. When the plain reaches sea level, it is called the base level. Volcanoes and earthquakes can create new mountains. When more mountains are created, the cycle starts again. This is called rejuvenation.

Davis came to be known as the father of American geography and a founder of geomorphology.

Washed Away

Erosion happens naturally, but it can also be caused by manmade factors, such as deforestation. Nearly 25 million acres (10 million hectares) of soil is being lost every year because of erosion.

Worldwide, soil is being swept away as fast as 10 to 40 times more than than it is being replenished. It takes eight years for a single acre (0.4 hectares) of soil to be replaced naturally. About 60 percent of soil that is washed away by erosion ends up in rivers, streams, and lakes. This makes these waterways more prone to flooding and contamination from pesticides in the soil.

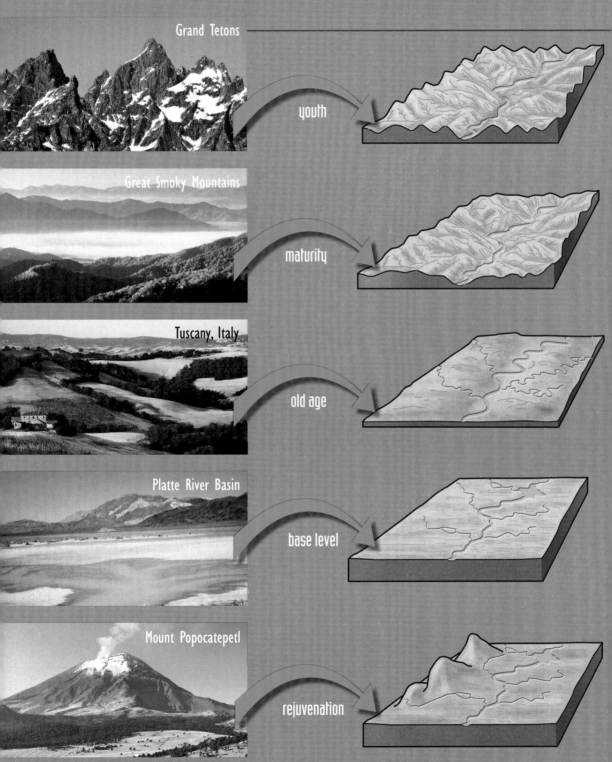

Grand Tetons

youth

Great Smoky Mountains

maturity

Tuscany, Italy

old age

Platte River Basin

base level

Mount Popocatepetl

rejuvenation

Albrecht Penck (1858-1945)

Albrecht Penck was an earth scientist who dedicated himself to the study of landforms. He also thought maps could be better, and he set out to improve them.

Penck was a German geologist and university science professor in Vienna and Berlin from 1885 to 1927. In Berlin he was also the director of the Institute and Museum for Oceanography. Penck's focus was glaciers and their effects on landforms. He studied two main types of glaciers: valley glaciers and continental glaciers. He was interested in how the force of gravity causes glaciers to move down from mountaintops into valleys.

Continental glaciers cover large areas of land and drastically change landforms. Today the only continental glaciers on Earth cover much of Greenland and Antarctica.

Penck's study of glaciers was significant, but he is probably best known for encouraging the creation of accurate geological maps. Since cartographers at that time used different styles and scales, it was

difficult to compare one map with another. Penck proposed that all maps have a scale of one to 1 million (1:1,000,000). This is called the representative fraction scale. Using the RF scale, 1 cm=10 km and 1 inch=15.8 miles. He believed that maps should be consistent all over the world.

At the fifth International Geographical Conference in 1891, he recommended a worldwide system of maps. He called it the International Map of the World. But it was 1913 before his idea took shape in what was called the Millionth Map of the World project. It was named this because it used the one-to-one-millionth scale.

Continental glacier in Greenland (top) and valley glacier in Canada

Scientists working on the Millionth Map of the World project also decided to use the Roman alphabet for all maps. This meant that countries with other alphabets would have to translate them into the Roman alphabet. They also agreed on standard colors. Towns, railroads, and boundaries would be in black. Roads would be red, and land features would be brown.

Each country was supposed to create its own map of itself. But this caused many problems. Not every country could afford to do so, nor did they all have mapmakers who could do it. Some countries took longer than others to finish their maps. Many maps were outdated by the time others were finished. By the 1980s, only about one-third of the maps of the countries were made.

Even though the project ended, many people thought that Penck's idea had merit.

Collecting Maps

Often mapmakers do not date their maps or globes. One reason is so the maps do not appear outdated, even if they are. Maps depicting old boundary and name changes can be worth quite a bit to collectors.

The Library of Congress' Geography and Map Division is the largest map collection in the world. It holds more than 4 million maps, 57,000 atlases, and 9,000 reference works. The library adds around 60,000 new map-related items to the collection every year.

23

Florence Bascom (1862-1945)

Florence Bascom was the first female geologist hired by the United States Geological Survey. But that was not the only "first" that Bascom accomplished in her career. She was the first woman to break the gender barrier at Johns Hopkins University, receiving a Ph.D. in geology in 1893. In class she had to sit behind a screen so she wouldn't distract the male students.

Another first for Bascom was her presentation of a scientific paper at the Geological Society of Washington. No other woman had ever presented to the society before. She also became the first woman to hold an office with the Geological Society of America.

Bascom was born in 1862 in Williamstown, Massachusetts. She became interested in geology as a young child, inspired by long rides with her father and his friend, a geology teacher. Her father, a university president, encouraged her to study geology.

She became an expert on rocks in the plateau region of the Eastern United States. She used her knowledge of rocks to learn how the Appalachian Mountains were formed and to make maps. Along with her job at the USGS, Bascom taught geology at Bryn Mawr College. Several of her students were hired by the USGS.

Clingmans Dome, in Tennessee's Great Smoky Mountains National Park, is the third-highest mountain in the Appalachian range.

Ellen Churchill Semple (1863–1932)

Ellen Churchill Semple is often regarded as America's first influential female geographer. Although her bachelor's degree from Vassar College in New York was in history, she was particularly interested in geography.

Semple was born January 8, 1863, in Louisville, Kentucky. As a child she was especially fascinated with books about history and travel. After graduating from college, she taught school for a while and also earned a master's degree. But then she heard about an outstanding geography professor at the University of Leipzig in Germany. In 1891 28-year-old Semple traveled to Germany to be taught by Friedrich Ratzel.

She lived with a German family so she could learn to speak the German language. At that time, German universities didn't allow women to enroll or graduate. So Semple just sat in on the classes, learning all she could. She never earned a degree in geography.

When Semple returned to America, she began researching, writing articles, and giving lectures. She was especially interested in the hills of Kentucky and the people who lived there. She showed how geography affects the way people live.

Although Semple spent time translating the works of German geographers into English, she also wrote books of her own. She was then appointed associate editor of the *Journal of Geography*, and two years later became a geography professor at the University of Chicago. She eventually taught at England's Oxford University and Clark University in Massachusetts.

Despite the obstacles, Semple succeeded at becoming an important geographer.

Rachel Carson dreamed of being a writer. When she was 10 years old, one of her stories was published. But it was a combination of her writing and a love of nature that made her influential in launching the environmental movement.

Carson was raised on a small farm in Pennsylvania, where she explored ponds and forests. In college she earned a degree in zoology, the study of animal life. She worked as a biologist for the U.S. Bureau of Fisheries. To add to her income, she began writing about science, particularly the beauty and wonder of the ocean. Her books *The Sea Around Us* and *The Edge of the Sea* encouraged others to appreciate and enjoy nature.

In the 1950s, she focused on the negative effects that pesticides were having on the environment. Pesticides were used to kill insects, but they were also damaging plant and animal life.

Carson's research led to *Silent Spring*, a book that shocked the world with its alarming description of what pesticides were doing to animal and plant life. It launched the American environmental movement and led to a nationwide ban of harmful pesticides. It also led to the formation of the Environmental Protection Agency.

Did You Know?

It took Carson four years to complete *Silent Spring*.

Geologist: Diane Evans (1954-)

NASA's Jet Propulsion Laboratory

Geologist Diane Evans' goal in her job with NASA's Jet Propulsion Laboratory is to improve life here on Earth. But she's not a typical geologist. She studies Earth from the information she receives from satellites and specialized telescopes in space. Evans' work also takes her all over the world to examine parts of Earth up close.

Evans became interested in geology while working at Yellowstone National Park the summer after her first year in college. "I was amazed by the bubbling mud pots and wanted to learn more about what caused them," she said. "I started taking geology courses when I returned to school in the fall and found them to be the

Modern-Day Exploration

Explorers of old crossed unknown lands on horseback to discover what was on Earth. Today an explorer might hitch a ride to the International Space Station, a research facility being assembled in space. It is the largest orbiting spacecraft in history. Up to seven astronauts man the station.

Explorers today also go into the ocean. The Aquarius Undersea Laboratory is the only underwater research lab in the world. Scientists who live and work onboard study landforms of the ocean floor in the Florida Keys.

most interesting classes I'd ever had."

At NASA Evans studies the information sent to Earth from satellites in space. "Satellites give a wide view, so you can see patterns," she said. In satellite photographs, Evans looks for giant cracks in the ground. They could be signs of coming earthquakes.

Evans also observes patterns in the oceans that might give her information about climate change. Satellites also "see" things that are normally invisible, such as the temperature and depth of the ocean.

Being There

If you were a geologist, you would study Earth's rocks and soil. Some other jobs you might have include ...
- Looking for underground mineral deposits
- Learning how to clean up contaminated soil
- Studying how to prevent landslides

For You to Do

Imagine what patterns or shapes you might see if you flew high above your town or city. Think about what the roads, rivers, buildings, and parks would look like from space. Now try drawing a map of what you imagined.

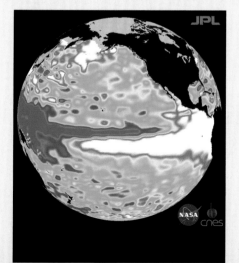

surface cracks on Earth

sea surface height

Earth Scientists at a Glance

Florence Bascom

Field of study: *Geology*

Known as: *First female geologist hired by the U.S. Geological Survey*

Nationality: *American*

Birthplace: *Williamstown, Massachusetts*

Date of birth: *July 14, 1862*

Date of death: *March 7, 1945*

Awards and honors: *First woman to receive a Ph.D. in geology from Johns Hopkins University, 1893; first woman elected to the council of the Geological Society of America, 1924*

Rachel Carson

Fields of study: *Marine biology, ecology, pesticides*

Known as: *Mother of the environmental movement; author of* Silent Spring

Nationality: *American*

Birthplace: *Springdale, Pennsylvania*

Date of birth: *May 27, 1907*

Date of death: *April 14, 1964*

Awards and honors: *Presidential Medal of Freedom, 1980; Rachel Carson Conservation Park and Rachel Carson National Wildlife Refuge named for her*

William Morris Davis

Field of study: *Engineering*

Known as: *Father of American geography; studied cycle of erosion*

Nationality: *American*

Birthplace: *Philadelphia, Pennsylvania*

Date of birth: *February 12, 1850*

Date of death: *February 5, 1934*

Awards and honors: *Founder of the Association of American Geographers, 1904; president of the association, 1904, 1905, 1909*

Diane Evans

Field of study: *Geology*

Known as: *Director of Earth Science and Technology directorate, NASA's Jet Propulsion Laboratory*

Nationality: *American*

Birthplace: *Euclid, Ohio*

Birth year: *1954*

Awards and honors: *NASA Outstanding Leadership Medal and Group Achievement Awards; Aviation Week and Space Technology Laurels Award For Outstanding Achievement in the Field of Space; International Technical Publications Competition Award of Excellence; IEEE Geoscience and Remote Sensing Transactions Prize Paper Award*

Grove Karl Gilbert

Fields of study: *Geology, geomorphology*

Known for: Report on the Geology of the Henry Mountains *and* Glaciers and Glaciation

Nationality: *American*

Birthplace: *Rochester, New York*

Date of birth: *May 6, 1843*

Date of death: *May 1, 1918*

Awards and honors: *Senior geologist for USGS, 1879; director of the USGS, 1881; Wollaston Medal, 1900; Daly Medal from the American Geographical Society, 1910; craters on the moon and on Mars named for him*

Gerardus Mercator

Field of study: *Cartography*

Known for: *Mercator projection (map projection); Mercator chart (navigation tool); technique for making globes*

Nationality: *Flemish*

Birthplace: *Rupelmonde, Flanders (now in Belgium)*

Date of birth: *March 5, 1512*

Date of death: *December 2, 1594*

Awards and honors: *Imperial seal of approval from Emperor Charles V, 1545; court cosmographer to Duke Wilhelm of Cleves, 1565*

John Muir

Field of study: *Engineering*

Known as: *Founder of Sierra Club; influenced the modern environmental movement*

Nationality: *Scottish-American*

Birthplace: *Dunbar, East Lothian, Scotland*

Date of birth: *April 21, 1838*

Date of death: *December 24, 1914*

Awards and honors: *Muir Glacier, John Muir Wilderness, Muir Woods National Monument, and the John Muir asteroid named for him; inducted into the California Hall of Fame, 2006*

Albrecht Penck

Field of study: *Geology*
Known for: *Study of glaciers*
Nationality: *German*
Birthplace: *Leipzig, Germany*
Date of birth: *September 25, 1858*
Date of death: *March 7, 1945*

Awards and honors: *Professor of geography at the University of Vienna, 1885–1906, and the University of Berlin, 1906–1927; glacier named for him*

John Wesley Powell

Field of study: *Explorer*
Known for: *Powell geographic expedition, exploration through Grand Canyon*
Nationality: *American*
Birthplace: *Mount Morris, New York*
Date of birth: *March 24, 1834*
Date of death: *September 23, 1902*

Awards and honors: *Secretary of the Illinois Natural History Society, 1859; director of USGS, 1881–1894; Lake Powell on the Colorado River named for him*

Ellen Churchill Semple

Field of study: *Geography*
Known as: *America's first influential female geographer*
Nationality: *American*
Birthplace: *Louisville, Kentucky*
Date of birth: *January 8, 1863*
Date of death: *May 8, 1932*

Awards and honors: *Associate editor of the* Journal of Geography, *1904; member of the Association of American Geographers, 1904; elected president of the association, 1921; honorary doctorate in law from the University of Kentucky, 1923*

4000 B.C. People in the Middle East begin to mine minerals such as tin, clay, iron ore, gold, and copper

540 B.C. Greek philosopher Xenophanes describes fossils of fish and shells found in mountain rock

400s B.C. Greek philosopher Empedocles says four elements—fire, air, earth, and water—form all other substances

1086 A.D. The *Dream Pool Essays* by Chinese scientist and statesman Shen Kua describe the principles of erosion, uplift, and sedimentation—the foundations of earth science

1452 Italian artist Leonardo da Vinci is born; recognizes that fossil shells are the remains of once-living organisms

1546 German physician and scientist Georgius Agricola introduces the word *fossil*

1638 Danish geologist Nicolas Steno is born; discovers a fossil of a shark's tooth and studies rock strata

1743 British physician and scientist Christopher Packe makes a geological map of the southeast portion of England

1760 British geologist and astronomer John Michell proposes that earthquakes are caused by one rock layer rubbing against another

1774 German geologist Abraham Werner introduces a classification of minerals

1775	The categorization of geology as a branch of science begins
1785	Scottish geologist James Hutton presents his paper, *Theory of the Earth*, in which he suggests that Earth is very old
1799	English geologist William Smith publishes *Order of the Strata*, and states that the same rock strata can be found in different regions, that they always lie in the same order, and that each kind of rock contains fossils from the same time period
1809	American geologist William Maclure, called the father of American geology, completes the first geological survey of the eastern United States
1812	German geologist and minerologist Friedrich Mohs creates the Mohs scale to measure the hardness of minerals
1815	William Smith creates the first large-scale geological map of England and Wales
1830	Scottish geologist Charles Lyell publishes his book, *Principles of Geology*, in which he states that the world is several hundred million years old
1903	English astronomer George Darwin and Irish physicist John Joly realize that radioactivity is partly responsible for Earth's heat
1907	American chemist Bertram Boltwood uses uranium to determine the age of rocks
1911	British geologist Arthur Holmes uses radioactivity to date rocks

1912	German geologist Alfred Wegener puts forward the continental drift theory, that the continents were once joined together as a single landmass
1935	American physicist Charles Richter develops the Richter scale to measure the intensity of earthquakes
1951	The Mariana Trench, the deepest part of the ocean and the deepest location on Earth, is first surveyed; it is 6.85 miles (11 km) deep and 44 miles (71 km) wide
1953	American geologist Bruce Heezen maps the Mid-Atlantic Ridge, a mountainlike ridge that extends through the Atlantic Ocean
1977	Deep-sea vents are discovered around the Galapagos Islands
1990	Oldest portion of the Pacific plate is found
2007	American geologist Vicki Hansen hypothesizes that early meteorites created the first rifts in Earth's crust, which in turn started plate tectonics
2009	Scientists declare that an Indonesian mud volcano eruption was caused by a drilling accident; the volcano caused more than 60,000 people to lose their homes

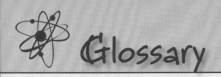

Glossary

base level—lowest level that water can erode a landform; sea level

block diagram—three-dimensional cutaway diagram

cartography—skill or technique of making maps

cycle of erosion—model for stream erosion proposed by William Morris Davis in the late 1800s

deforestation—cutting down or destruction of forests

dune—hill or ridge of wind-blown sand

earthquake—sudden movement of Earth's crust caused by the release of stress along tectonic plate boundaries

erosion—condition in which Earth's surface is worn away by the action of water, wind, and air

geography—study of Earth and its features

geologist—person who studies geology

geomorphology—study of landforms and the forces and processes that form them

glacier—large mass of ice slowly moving over land

gorge—deep, narrow passage with steep rocky sides

gravity—force that pulls objects toward Earth's center

landform—natural formation on Earth's surface, such as plains, plateaus, valleys, and mountains

map projection—display of a globe onto a flat map

monolith—tall block of solid stone standing by itself

national parks—areas of land chosen by a government and given special protection

natural resource—any substance found in nature that people use, such as soil, air, trees, coal, and oil

observatory—buildings designed to study outer space

pesticide—substances, usually chemical, applied to crops to kill harmful insects and other creatures

plateau—landform that has high elevation and a level surface

rejuvenation—process of new mountains forming at base level

seismograph—instrument used to measure and record motions in Earth's crust, especially intensity and duration of earthquakes

tsunami—gigantic ocean wave created by an undersea earthquake, landslide, or volcanic eruption

volcano—vents in Earth's crust from which lava pours; mountains formed from the buildup of lava

Additional Resources

Fradin, Dennis, and Judy Fradin. *Witness to Disaster: Earthquakes*. Washington, D.C.: National Geographic Children's Books, 2008.

Harrison, David L. *Mountains: The Tops of the World*. Honesdale, Pa.: Boyds Mills Press, 2005.

Hooper, Meredith. *The Island That Moved: How Shifting Forces Shape Our Earth*. New York: Viking, 2004.

Rubin, Ken. *Volcanoes & Earthquakes*. New York: Simon & Schuster Children's Publishing, 2007.

Stille, Darlene. *Plate Tectonics: Earth's Moving Crust*. Minneapolis: Compass Point Books, 2007.

Yep, Laurence. *The Earth Dragon Awakes: The San Francisco Earthquake of 1906*. New York: HarperCollins, 2008.

Internet Sites

FactHound offers a safe, fun way to find Internet sites related to this book. All of the sites on FactHound have been researched by our staff.

Here's all you do:

Visit *www.facthound.com*

FactHound will fetch the best sites for you!

Index

Lynn Van Gorp

Lynn Van Gorp graduated with a master of science degree from the University of Calgary, Canada, and did additional graduate work at the University of Washington, Seattle, and the University of California, Irvine. She has taught for more than 30 years at the elementary and middle school levels and at the university level. Her education focus areas include science, reading, and technology. She has written a number of student- and teacher-based curriculum-related publications.

Image Credits

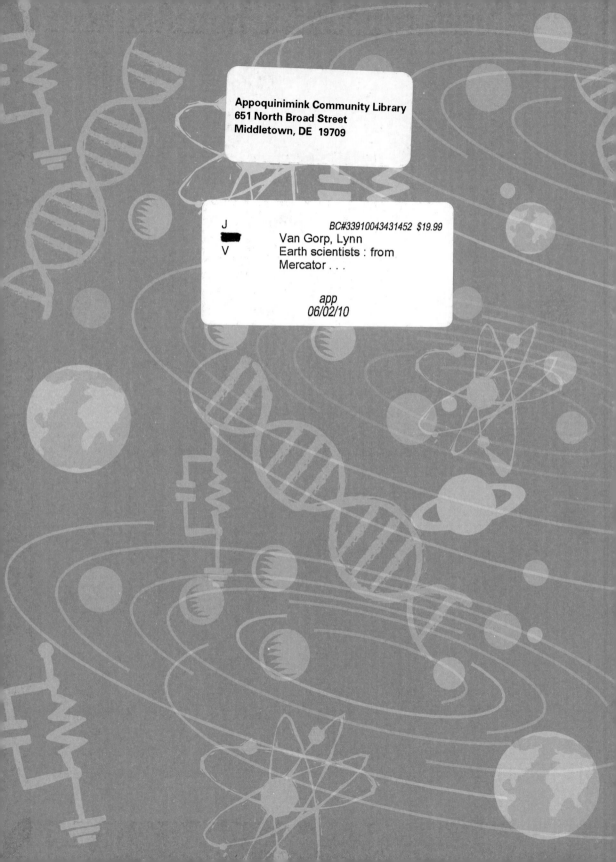